LIFE IN THE SEA

written by Christina Wilsdon
reviewed by Robert E. Budliger

Reader's Digest
Children's Books®

Pleasantville, New York • Montréal, Québec • Bath, United Kingdom

What Lives in the Ocean?

Fish as big as buses, animals that look like flowers, eight-legged creatures that squirt ink—these are just a few of the amazing animals that live in the ocean.

The ocean is home to more than 200,000 kinds of animals, plants, and one-celled living things. Some scientists think a million or more species will be discovered in the next few years.

Some ocean animals are big and well known—like sharks, whales, dolphins, tuna, and lobsters. But the ocean is also filled with living things that are so tiny, a dozen of them could sit on a dime with room to spare. Others are even smaller and can be seen only with a microscope.

Did You Know?

Scientists recently found about 20,000 kinds of microscopic living things in just 1 quart of ocean water—an amount of water that would only half fill a large soda bottle.

Floating Life

A layer of very tiny living things, called **plankton**, floats in the upper part of the ocean. The plantlike plankton use sunlight to make their food, just as plants on land do. The tiny animal plankton eat the plantlike ones.

What's That Word?

As you read, you will see words that are in **bold** type. Look for them in the glossary on page 22 to learn what they mean.

Lots of Arms

Octopuses and squid are eight-armed animals found only in saltwater. Their arms are lined with rows of suction cups called suckers. These animals can wriggle their way along the seabed with their arms, as well as cling to rocks with their suckers.

Squid also have two tentacles that are usually longer than their arms. They use the tentacles to catch fish and shrimp.

Suckers and long arms come in handy for grabbing **prey**, too. An octopus drags its prey to its mouth, which is at the base of its arms. It has a beak as sharp and strong as a parrot's for biting its prey.

Octopuses and squid have several ways to protect themselves. One way is to speed away from a **predator** by taking water into its body, then pushing it out through a funnel-shaped part called a siphon. This action is called **jetting**.

Most octopuses and many squid can change the color, pattern, and texture of their skin in the blink of an eye! They change color to blend in with their background so they won't be noticed by predators.

Did You Know?

If an octopus loses one of its arms, it can grow a new one.

Inked Out

An octopus or a squid can flee a predator by shooting out a cloud of dark ink into the water. The ink hides it and startles the predator, giving the octopus or squid a head start on its getaway.

Some Thing's Fishy

What does a fish have inside it that an octopus doesn't? A skeleton. Fish have a backbone and other bones just as you do. All fish have this in common, even if they are shaped quite differently. A tuna looks nothing like a sea horse, but they are both fish.

Fish breathe underwater using a pair of organs called **gills**. The gills get oxygen from the water as it flows through them.

Almost all fish have fins on their bodies. The tail fins point up and down. Most fish swim by waving their bodies from side to side so that its tail wags and its fins push against the water.

Some fish, such as the tuna, have very stiff, pointed tail fins for going extra-fast. A tuna doesn't wave its body from side to side as it swims—its power is in its tail.

Did You Know?

A flounder starts life as a fish with an eye on each side of its head. But as it grows, one eye slowly moves over next to the other eye. The fish also starts living sideways. Being a flatfish lets a flounder lie flat on the seabed, where it blends in with sand and stones.

Coral Reef Fish

Some of the ocean's most colorful fish live in places called coral reefs. The longhorn cowfish's yellow body is boxy and hard. Only big fish with strong jaws can eat it. The harlequin tuskfish has blue teeth!

Longhorn Cowfish

Harlequin Tuskfish

The boldly colored clown fish avoids predators by tucking itself among the stinging tentacles of flowerlike animals called anemones. The clown fish's skin oozes a slime that protects it from the stings, but other fish must keep away. It's no surprise, then, that the clown fish is also known as the anemonefish.

Shore Leave

Like many people, you probably picture a shark as a fierce animal with huge, toothy jaws. But sharks come in many shapes and sizes—and some of them aren't a bit fierce.

The world's biggest fish is a shark that is so gentle that divers can stroke its back. It is the whale shark. A whale shark can be up to 40 feet long—a little longer than a big school bus. It swims slowly, filtering plankton and small fish from the water. Basking sharks and megamouth sharks feed this way, too.

Most sharks are torpedo-shaped and are swift swimmers. Some have different shapes. The angel shark has a wide, flat body with large, winglike side fins.

A hammerhead shark has a head shaped like a hammer, with its eyes at either end. Its wide head helps it find food. Some hammerheads even use their heads to dig up food or hold down struggling prey.

Did You Know?

Sharks do not have bony skeletons as other fish do. Their skeletons are made of **cartilage,** the same flexible material found in your ears and the tip of your nose.

The Great White

The most famous shark is the great white. It is one of the biggest sharks. It can grow to be about 23 feet long. Great whites eat fish, sea turtles, seals, and dead animals, as well as other sharks. This kind of shark is feared because it is known to attack people.

The usually harmless blacktip reef shark is named for the dark tips on all its fins.

A Sharp Cookie!

The little cookie-cutter shark has big, sharp teeth. It feeds by "kissing" the side of a bigger animal, then sticking to it with its suction-cup lips. Next, it chews a rounded bite out of it. Squid, dolphins, and even whales have scars that show they've been chomped by cookie-cutters.

Rays and Skates

Rays and skates are strange, flat fish with fins like bat wings. They are the sharks' closest relatives. Like sharks, they have skeletons made of cartilage. But instead of being shaped like submarines, most rays and skates look more like flying carpets flapping through the ocean. Scientists call the wide, flat side fins "wings."

Most rays and skates feed on the seafloor. They skim above the sand and mud like metal detectors on the prowl, eating snails, clams, shrimp, and fish without shells.

The biggest ray is the giant manta ray. Its wings measure about 20 feet from tip to tip. It can weigh more than 3,500 pounds— almost as much as three milk cows. This huge ray eats plankton that it filters from the water. It waves plankton toward its mouth with the two fins that stick out from its head like horns.

Zap!

An electric ray makes electricity in organs that are located behind its eyes, near the base of its side fins. It uses the electricity to stun fish, which it eats. The biggest electric ray is the Atlantic torpedo ray. It can be as long as a tall adult human and produce shocks strong enough to stun a diver.

Did You Know?

Rays and skates are members of a group that scientists call batoids. Batoids have fins that look like the wings of bats. Sawfish and guitarfish also belong to this special group of sea creatures.

The eagle ray slowly flaps its large, triangle-shaped wings up and down to push itself through the water.

Turtles of the Sea

The ocean is home to seven kinds of turtles. Sea turtles hatch on land but spend the rest of their lives in the ocean.

A female sea turtle crawls out of the ocean onto a beach when she is ready to lay eggs. Using her hind feet, she digs a hole. Then she lays the eggs inside it and buries them before she heads back to sea.

The baby turtles hatch many weeks later. As soon as they pop out of the sand, they scramble toward the ocean. Some are caught and eaten by crabs and other predators. The rest swim away.

The biggest sea turtle is the leatherback. It can be up to 8 feet long—about the length of a big couch. It weighs about 1,100 pounds—about as much as a riding horse. The leatherback is named for the thick skin on its back, which is stuck full of little bony plates. Other sea turtles have shells covered with broad, tough shields.

Did You Know?

A single loggerhead turtle may have as many as 100 kinds of animals and plantlike living things on its shell! These stowaways include barnacles, tiny shrimplike animals, and algae.

Jaws!

The jaws of sea turtles are clues to what they eat. A green sea turtle, like this one, has jaws that are jagged like a bread knife, just right for grazing on seaweed and turtle grass. A  loggerhead has strong, sharp jaws for eating animals with shells, such as sea snails, or tough outer skeletons, such as crabs. A leatherback has a hooked jaw and backward-pointing spines in its throat so that slippery jellyfish and squid can't slide out of its mouth.

A female leatherback will swim more than 1,500 miles just to lay her eggs on the same beach where she was born.

What Is a Whale?

A whale looks a lot like a fish, but it is not. A whale is a **mammal**—a **warm-blooded** animal that has hair. A female mammal makes milk for her young. A whale does not have gills for breathing. It has a **blowhole** on top of its head and must come to the surface to breathe air. A thick layer of fat under the skin, called blubber, keeps whales warm in the ocean.

Scientists divide whales into two groups—toothed whales and **baleen** whales. A toothed whale has teeth. Sperm whales, narwhals, and belugas are toothed whales. A baleen whale has no teeth. Instead, it has long strips of tough material hanging from its upper jaw inside its mouth. This material is called baleen. A baleen whale strains mouthfuls of water through its baleen to filter out food.

The biggest whale, the blue whale, feeds on tiny plankton animals called **krill** that look like tiny shrimp. A blue whale may eat up to 16,000 pounds of krill in just one day. On this meal plan, the whale can grow to weigh 200,000 pounds!

The White Whale

The cold Arctic Ocean is home to white whales called belugas. Belugas are gray when they are born and turn white as they grow. Unlike other whales, they can easily turn their heads on their flexible necks.

Both the gray whale (far left) and the sei whale (center) are baleen whales that feed on plankton. The black-and-white killer whale, or orca (near left), is a toothed whale that eats much bigger food, such as seals, sharks, and sea lions.

Finned, Not Fishy

Dolphins and porpoises are toothed whales. Sometimes they can be seen leaping in and out of the water, as if stitching their way through the waves. This motion is called **porpoising.**

By porpoising, a dolphin or porpoise can swim faster, because it is easier to move forward through air than through water. Each leap also lets the animal take a breath before diving back underwater.

Seals, sea lions, and walruses are ocean mammals that also spend time on land. A seal is graceful at sea, zooming through the water to catch fish. On land, it shuffles along on its belly, dragging its hind flippers. A sea lion has an easier time walking onshore than most seals do because it can rotate its hind flippers forward, then waddle on all four flippers.

Killer Whales

The biggest dolphins, the orcas, eat sharks, turtles, dolphins, porpoises, and other whales. This menu gives orcas their other name—killer whales. Orcas can grow to be as long as a big school bus. They are the fastest swimmers among sea mammals. An orca can zip along at a speed of 40 miles an hour.

Walruses
A walrus uses its big tusks like ski poles to pull itself onto the shore or a floating piece of ice.

Dolphins like these Pacific white-sided dolphins jump high into the air and then belly flop onto the water's surface. This is called breaching.

Seeing Seabirds

Gulls, puffins, terns, and other seabirds spend much of their lives flying over the ocean and feeding from it. Some visit land only to lay eggs and raise their young.

Many seabirds have huge wings that help them soar for long stretches of time. The biggest wingspan belongs to the wandering albatross. This bird's wings measure up to 12 feet from tip to tip—as much as four yardsticks laid end to end.

An albatross rarely needs to flap its wings because wind blows almost nonstop across the Southern Ocean. If the wind dies, the albatross floats in the water until the wind starts to blow again. An albatross can fly thousands of miles a year as it looks around the South Pole for squid and fish to eat.

Did You Know?

Sooty shearwaters hold the record for the longest **migration.** They fly from New Zealand, where they nest, to feeding areas in the North Pacific, then back to New Zealand. That is almost 40,000 miles in one year—a distance that is nearly twice around the planet Earth!

Some birds dive headfirst into the water from high in the air to catch fish. They fold their wings, point their bills toward the ocean, and enter the water like darts. This is called plunge-diving. Gannets and brown pelicans hunt this way. Other seabirds, like storm petrels, flap just above the ocean's surface, dabbing their feet in the water as they snatch up tiny animals.

An albatross takes one mate for its entire life, which can be from 50 to 80 years long.

Birds That Can't Fly

Penguins are seabirds that can't fly in the air but fly fast and deep in the water, flapping furiously as they chase fish. The biggest penguin is the emperor penguin, which lives in Antarctica.

Glossary

baleen: Strips of tough material hanging from a whale's upper jaw that filter food from water

blowhole: A hole at the top of a dolphin's or whale's head that lets the animal breathe air in and out

cartilage: The rubbery, flexible material that forms the skeleton of sharks, rays, and skates

gills: Body parts on fish that absorb oxygen from water

jetting: Shooting out water to move quickly away from danger

krill: Tiny shrimplike ocean animals in plankton

mammal: A warm-blooded animal that has hair (at some stage of its life) and feeds its young milk produced by the mother

migration: The regular trip from one place to another from season to season

plankton: Tiny living things that float mainly in the ocean's upper layers

porpoising: A way some dolphins swim by leaping out of the water in low curves, allowing them to take a quick breath of air while swimming

predator: An animal that eats other animals

prey: Animals that are eaten by other animals

warm-blooded: Having a body temperature that stays the same when the temperature of the habitat changes